OUR LIVING PLANET

Land

BLACKBIRCH®
PRESS

THOMSON
GALE

San Diego • Detroit • New York • San Francisco • Cleveland
New Haven, Conn. • Waterville, Maine • London • Munich

THOMSON

GALE

For more information, contact
The Gale Group, Inc.
27500 Drake Rd.
Farmington Hills, MI 48331-3535
Or you can visit our Internet site at http://www.gale.com

Adapted by A S Publishing from
El Paisaje © Parromon Ediciones S.A. 1996

Text: Miquel Àngel Gilbert
Illustrations: Lidia di Blasi
Design: Beatriz Seoane

Every effort has been made to trace the owners of copyrighted material.

LIBRARY OF CONGRESS CATALOGING-IN-PUBLICATION DATA

Gilbert, Miquel Àngel.
   Land / by Miquel Àngel Gilbert.
      v. cm. — (Living planet series)
   Contents: The living landscape — The shape of the land — Erosion — Climate and vegetation — Survival in the desert.
   ISBN 1-56711-668-X (hardback : alk. paper)
   1. Landforms—Juvenile literature. 2. Natural history—Juvenile literature. [1. Landforms. 2. Geology.] I. Title. II. Series.
   GB453 .G56 2003
   551.41—dc21   2002009530

Printed in Spain
10 9 8 7 6 5 4 3 2 1

CONTENTS

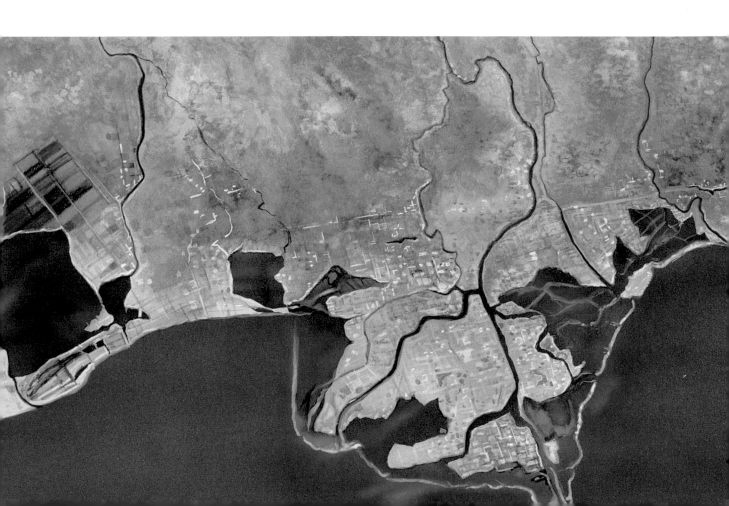

THE LIVING LANDSCAPE

What do you see when you look around you? City streets, open country, rolling hills, or the sea? The shape of the land depends mostly on the rock that lies beneath it. Over millions of years, natural processes have shaped the rock into what we see today: mountains or valleys, plains or hills, cliffs or sandy beaches. Climate shapes a landscape's surface features since it determines what plants and animals can live there.

Whatever the natural vegetation may be—forest, grassland, or scrub—nearly everywhere there will be animals. Most animals stay safely out of sight. Others, such as reindeer in the snowy Arctic tundra or eagles that soar high over rocky ledges, add a living presence to the landscape.

Human beings have made the most significant changes to the landscape. They have

The character of the landscape depends on the rocks beneath it, the plant and animal life that it supports, and the changes that people have made to it.

cut down forests, drained swamps, plowed grasslands, and altered the character of vast tracts of land throughout history. More recently, they have built dams, causing river valleys to flood. They have hacked out huge holes in the ground to get stone to build towns and roads.

The earth formed around 4,600 million years ago. Since then, the landscape has constantly changed.

PRECAMBRIAN 4600–590*   PALAEOZOIC 590–248   * Millions of years ago

MESOZOIC   Triassic 248–213   Jurassic 213–144   Cretaceous 144–65

Continents are continuously moving they inch apart or together in different parts of the world. The shape of the land changes, too. Mountain ranges that were once tall are now mere hills. Climates have changed. Several times, the world has grown so cold that ice sheets have spread across lands that are now tropical. Throughout time, animals and plants have evolved.

People have been on earth for a relatively short length of time. Before they appeared, other animals dominated the earth. We know about them from their fossils, which are traces of living things left in rocks. Geologists use fossils to identify the ages of rocks.

Scientists divide time into eras and periods. In Precambrian times, life was confined to the sea. During the Paleozoic era, fish evolved, followed by amphibians and reptiles. During the Mesozoic era, dinosaurs ruled the earth. Mammals, including human beings, became dominant during the Cenozoic, the era in which we live.

Life forms and landscapes constantly evolve. The climate is one of the most important influences.

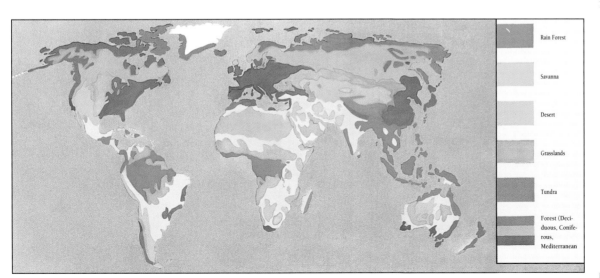

Rain Forest

Savanna

Desert

Grasslands

Tundra

Forest (Deciduous, Coniferous, Mediterranean

THE SHAPE OF THE LAND

Mountains and lakes, rolling hills, flat plains, and rocky outcrops are features of a landscape that is always changing. The earth's surface is cracked into plates, which float on a layer of semi-molten rock. Forces in this layer cause the plates to move. In some places, they collide; in others, they move apart. Where they collide, the land may buckle up into mountains, called fold mountains.

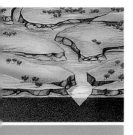

The shape of the land is created by forces within the earth, but is continually changed by the actions of weathering, water, and other natural agents on the surface.

As fast as mountains form, they begin to be broken down by natural forces. Rain, wind, frost, and ice carve the rocky surface into a variety of shapes, and over millions of years, these forces wear it flat. Rivers carve valleys and carry the broken rock particles, called sediment, to the sea. The sediment settles in layers on the seabed. In time, sediment forms new rock that may later be raised up by the earth's movements.

In some places, when plates meet head-on or move past each other, the rocks do not fold but break. These breaks are called faults. The rocks on each side of the fault may be forced either up or down. When two faults occur parallel to each other, the rock between them may be forced up to form a flat-topped block mountain, or it may be forced down to form a rift valley. Sometimes, parts of the valley fill with water to form lakes.

Sudden movements along a fault can cause catastrophic earthquakes. Many severe quakes occur along transform faults, where two moving plates have jammed together. The pressure mounts, until suddenly the rocks snap and the plates shift with a jerk.

Volcanoes also occur where plates move against each other. Magma pours out of volcanoes as lava. It solidifies into new rock, and in time, builds up into mountains. Where plates move apart under the sea, magma wells up to form new rock. In some places, the edge of one plate slides down under another into the magma, and the rock is destroyed. The continuous destruction of old rock and emergence of new rock is called the rock cycle.

Earth's movements create mountains, rivers carve valleys, and rocks are worn down and carried to the sea.

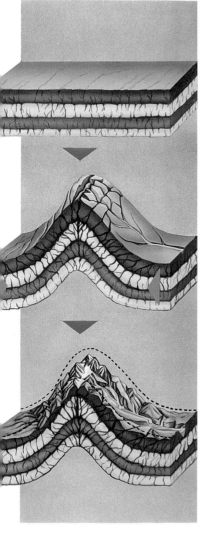

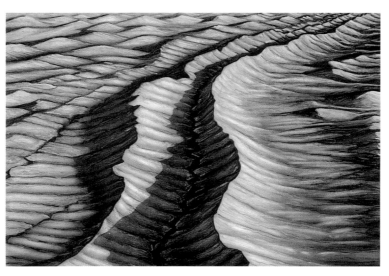

EROSION

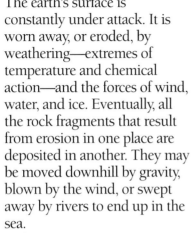

The earth's surface is constantly under attack. It is worn away, or eroded, by weathering—extremes of temperature and chemical action—and the forces of wind, water, and ice. Eventually, all the rock fragments that result from erosion in one place are deposited in another. They may be moved downhill by gravity, blown by the wind, or swept away by rivers to end up in the sea.

On seacoasts, waves carrying sand and pebbles endlessly pound the shore. They cut into a cliff face and weaken its base. Eventually, the rock, soil, and vegetation on top collapse and leave a bare cliff. Where the rock is soft, the sea may carve caves. When waves pound both sides of a promontory, they may wear through the rock between two caves and cause a natural arch.

On land, the wind acts like a sandblaster. It picks up dust and sand and hurls it at rocks. Because the wind cannot lift the particles high, the rock is worn down more at ground level than higher up. This results in irregularly shaped formations.

On high mountains, the snow never melts. It builds up in layers many feet deep. The

Land surfaces are shaped by erosion. Rocks and soil either slide downhill or are carried down by wind, ice, or water.

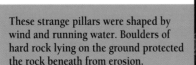

These strange pillars were shaped by wind and running water. Boulders of hard rock lying on the ground protected the rock beneath from erosion.

fresh snow weighs down on the snow underneath and compacts it into ice. As the ice thickens, it becomes heavier and begins to move downhill under its own weight. It becomes a river of ice called a glacier. Rocks embedded in the ice act as scrapers. They gouge out the surrounding rock into a steep-sided, U-shaped valley.

The scenery in many desert regions results from ancient glaciers and rivers. Rainstorms

swollen with rain—sweep downhill, they carry loose rocks that carve a V-shaped valley. The flowing river picks up pebbles, sand, and mud. Near the mouth of the river, the current slows, and the river gradually drops its load. The matter that reaches the sea is spread along the shore by sea currents to form beaches, some of which are backed by rows of dunes.

in deserts are rare, but they may be violent enough to cause instant rivers that sweep away the surface sand. Windblown sand continues the work of the rain, because it scours everything in its path. Hard rocks remain after softer rocks have been worn away, and leave a landscape of rounded rocks and isolated flat-topped hills.

Rivers often start where glaciers end. As torrents of melted snow—sometimes

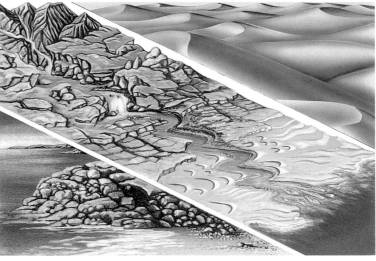

Near its source, a mountain torrent carves out a steep-sided, funnel-shaped valley, which is typical of mountain landscapes everywhere.

CLIMATE AND VEGETATION

During the ice ages, polar ice sheets spread out over the globe. While northern lands were covered with ice, places that are now hot and dry had mild, temperate climates. The Sahara Desert was warm enough to support wild animals, people, and cattle. Then, about 10,000 years ago, the climate became hotter. The ice melted, and the once fertile lands farther south eventually became desert.

The Sahara 5,000 years ago

Because of the curve of the earth, the sun's rays are most effective at the equator and less so at the poles.

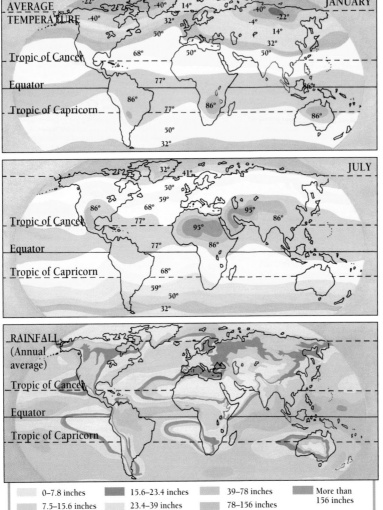

| 0–7.8 inches | 15.6–23.4 inches | 39–78 inches | More than 156 inches |
| 7.5–15.6 inches | 23.4–39 inches | 78–156 inches | |

The sun primarily determines climate. Near the equator, the sun is almost directly overhead, so the lands there receive the strongest sunlight. Near the poles, the sun's rays hit the earth at an angle that causes the rays to spread out over a greater area. Because the rays are spread over a larger area, the land is cooler. The heat from the ground at the equator warms the air, which makes it rise. The air is cooled as it rises. The water vapor in the cooled air condenses, and falls back to the earth as rain. The mass of air, now cool and dry, spreads out north and south of the equator. Around latitudes 30° N and 30° S, near the tropics of Cancer and Capricorn, the cool air sinks and becomes warmer as it descends. Warm air can hold more water vapor than cold air can, so there is no rainfall, and vast areas of land in those regions are hot desert.

Plants need water and sunlight to grow well, so the vegetation and animal life in any region depend on the climate. The equatorial climate is hot and wet all year long, so plants quickly grow thick and form dense rain forests. Desert climates are hot and dry all year. Few plants can grow in these conditions, so the land consists of bare rock or sand dunes shifting.

Climate is determined not only by distance from the equator but also by distance from the sea. Ocean currents increase or decrease the temperature of coastal lands. Water also warms up and cools down more slowly than does land. As a result, inland areas have warmer summers and colder winters with less rainfall. These conditions have created vast grassy plains with few trees.

Altitude also affects climate. Temperature falls by about 1.8°F (1°C) for every 328 feet (100 m) in elevation, so someone who travels up a mountain moves through increasingly cooler climates. The wettest areas are found on coasts, where predominant winds have traveled great distances over the sea. These winds drop their moisture as they rise over coastal mountains. The winds, then dry, continue on and cause deserts to form farther inland.

Plant life is vigorous and varied in areas of great heat and high rainfall.

THE ABUNDANT RAIN FORESTS

Emergents

Canopy

Understory

Forest floor

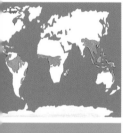

Tropical rain forests flourish at the equator, the only place where heat and water are available all year long.

Nowhere on earth is plant and animal life as abundant as in tropical rain forests. The plants grow close together because the water and warmth they need is available all year. The forest has several layers.

The tallest trees are called emergents. Under the emergents is a dense canopy of tree crowns, and below them is an understory of smaller trees, shrubs, and ferns. The lowest layer is the shady forest floor.

Woody vines called lianas clamber up the trees to reach the sunlight. These vines burst into leaf only when they reach the canopy.

Other forest plants, called epiphytes, never touch the ground. They root on high branches, where they live off nutrients dissolved in rainwater and on decayed leaves that drift down from the canopy above. Orchids are the most well-known epiphytes. Mosses, lichens, and fungi also grow on the other plants and on the forest floor.

Plant life in tropical rain forests is more diverse than anywhere else on earth. Scientists believe that about half of the world's estimated 4.5 million plant and animal species live in these hot, damp regions. In one square mile, 200 different trees may flourish. As many as 100 different kinds of plants may climb up or grow on a single tree. The Amazon Rain Forest in Brazil covers 2 million square miles (5.2 million sq km).

Rainforest soils tend to be infertile. Nutrients are quickly used by growing plants or washed away by the rain. The plants take their nourishment from the decayed vegetation that falls from the canopy. Even the tallest trees have shallow roots so that they can feed on the nutrients that lie on the ground.

The diversity of animal life in rain forests is as rich as that of the plants. One-tenth of the world's bird species live in the Brazilian forest, and about 2,500 types of fish swim in the Amazon River. The tree layers provide a variety of habitats. In the canopy, monkeys, snakes, and sloths move through the branches alongside parrots, toucans, and hummingbirds. On the ground there are ants, snakes, and armadillos, and big predators like the jaguar stalk through the trees. Insects are found at all levels.

Every time a giant forest tree falls, a gap opens in the canopy. Seeds lying dormant on the floor quickly take root and grow toward the precious sunlight.

THE SAVANNAS, HOME OF THE HERDS

Savannas are tropical grasslands with widely scattered trees and shrubs. They are the home of elephants and herds of other grazing animals that feed on clumps of grass and gather at water holes. Most savannas experience daytime temperatures that rarely fall below 68°F (20°C). Because the rainy season is short, the ability to get enough water is important for both plants and animals.

Savannas cover nearly 40 percent of Africa, and vast regions of South America and Australia

Baobab   Acacia

Savanna grass has thick blades that conserve moisture. In dry places, it is only a few inches high. In wetter areas, it may be 9.8 feet (3 m) high. There is too little water for most trees to grow, but acacia and baobab trees have ways to survive drought. The acacia has spiny leaves, and its roots go down deep to reach moisture in the ground. Baobabs store water in their huge, spongy trunks.

January	February	March	April	May	June	July	August	September	October	November	December

Every year, when the long dry season ends, huge fires sweep across the African savannas. The flames lick through the carpet of dead, brown grass.

Burning gives new life to the savanna. It stops trees that would otherwise spread at the expense of valuable grass. The ashes of the burned grass enrich the soil and help new grass to grow. The seeds and roots of the grasses are untouched by the flames. They are ready to spring to life again when the rains come. At that time, the daily downpours turn the grass green and let flowers bloom. Mature acacia trees that have survived the flames are covered with yellow blossoms.

Different animals graze the new grass in succession. Zebras bite off the coarse tops of the grasses. Wildebeests follow, and chew the lower, tender parts of the grass down to the ground. Finally, gazelles nibble the green shoots that spring from the base of the stems. Giraffes browse the trees above.

Every year, at certain times, the herds of the African savannas migrate to richer pastures. Often, they must travel hundreds of miles. Wherever they go, they are followed by the animals—such as lions, leopards, cheetahs, hyenas, and jackals—that prey on them.

Rainy seasons twice a year bring renewal to the parched, and often burned, grasslands. Animals migrate to take advantage of the fresh grass.

SURVIVAL IN THE DESERT

Hot deserts have an almost unbearable climate. Temperatures may rise to more than 100°F (38°C) by day and drop to the freezing point at night. Water is scarce or nonexistent. In parts of the Sahara in Africa and the Atacama Desert in South America, rain may not fall for years, and then a sudden storm may produce a flash flood. Life still manages to survive because both animals and plants have adapted to these conditions.

Some plants are drought evaders. Their seeds lie on the ground until rain comes. When enough rain falls, they spring into life. Within a few weeks, they will flower and scatter their seeds. Other plants are drought resisters. Cacti have long shallow roots that collect water over a large area to store in their fleshy stems. Their waxy skin and spines retain the moisture

Hot deserts occupy about one-seventh of the world's land surface. Many are "seas", of barren sand, but others support a variety of plants.

and make them hard for animals to eat.

Wind and water shape the desert surface. A quarter of the world's deserts are covered with sand that the winds pile up into dunes. Elsewhere, the winds sweep away the loose sand and leave bare rock. Rain from rare, but violent, cloudbursts scours deep, straight-sided valleys in the desert floor.

These normally dry riverbeds are called wadis or arroyos.

An oasis is a green and fertile place in the desert, where there is always enough water to keep plants and animals alive. The water comes from springs, underground streams, or wells. In some places, water from hills or mountains seeps through permeable rocks deep underground and then resurfaces. Date palms, with their highly nutritious fruit, commonly grow around oases in the deserts of North Africa.

At night, the desert comes alive. Lizards, snakes, and small mammals—such as kit foxes and kangaroo rats— hide under stones or in burrows during the day. They come out only in the cool of the night. They take care to avoid poisonous scorpions and snakes. The Arabian camel can go for a week without a drink of water. Fat in its hump gives it an indirect water supply.

When rain comes, millions of insects emerge from eggs and grubs. They must quickly breed and lay their eggs before they die from lack of moisture.

The animals in the picture below would not all be found in the same desert. Those to the left of the tall saguaro cactus come from North American deserts. Those on the right come from African and Asian deserts.

Many desert animals have adaptations that help them to survive. The fennec fox has big ears that give it excellent hearing for hunting at night. Its large ears also radiate heat and help to keep the fox cool in the daytime.

17

GRASSLANDS:
WHERE BISON ROAMED

The prairies of North America were once a sea of tall waving grasses where great herds of bison roamed. Today, much of the rolling plains are planted with wheat or corn. The prairies, the pampas of South America, the veld of southern Africa, and the steppes of Eurasia are the great temperate grasslands of the world. Like the savannas, they have a long dry season that restricts tree growth.

The grass grows as high as the rainfall allows. In the prairies, it may be 6.6 feet (2 m) tall. In steppe regions, it may be less than 9.8 inches (25 cm) high. Although summers are hot, winters are cold. The climate on the steppes is particularly harsh, with icy winters and torrid summers. Lack of water allows only short, often scanty, grass to grow.

PRAIRIE

The great grasslands lie in the heart of continents far from the sea.

STEPPE

The rich, dark soil of the prairies is more fertile than that of the steppes. It contains more humus, which forms like compost from the decay of vegetable material. The greater rainfall on the prairies allows more grass to grow. The natural decay of the grasses' long roots makes the soil fertile. The relatively thin vegetation of the steppe makes the soil thinner and poorer.

Only the least fertile and inhospitably cold areas of grassland retain their natural vegetation and wildlife today. Most have been turned into farmland. Wheat is grown on prairie and steppe alike, although the yield from prairies is greater. Where the land is not suitable for crops, cattle are grazed. The pampas and the veld have rich prairie soils suitable for growing crops and raising livestock.

Like the bison, most animals that live on the

PRAIRIE IN SUMMER

PRAIRIE IN WINTER

Most of the world's natural grasslands are now used to grow wheat or to graze cattle.

prairies are herbivores. The antelope-like pronghorn and the jackrabbit run to escape their enemies. The prairie dog stays safe in tunnels below the ground. Its holes are also used by the burrowing owl. The prairie chicken, a type of grouse, nests among the grasses. Insects, especially butterflies and grasshoppers, are everywhere.

THE NORTHERN FORESTS

Most of the world's temperate forests are in the northern hemisphere. Thousands of years ago, Europe was nearly one vast forest, as was much of northern North America and Asia. As soon as human beings developed tools, they began to cut down trees for firewood, timber, and farmland. Even so, much natural forest still remains.

The types of trees that grow vary with the climate. In the north are evergreen coniferous trees that can withstand long, bitter winters. To the south are broad-leaved deciduous trees that shed their leaves once a year.

In Mediterranean woodlands, the trees are mostly evergreens, with small tough leaves that can cope with strong summer sunlight and a shortage of water. Similar vegetation is found in California and coastal regions in the southern hemisphere.

Beneath the taller trees are bushes and shrubs, and below

them is undergrowth. In clearings, the sunlight enables a wealth of flowers to bloom. Unlike the oak trees that grow farther north, the cork oak has evergreen leaves. Its thick bark is used to make cork.

Many animals make their homes in undisturbed areas of the forest. The largest are the deer. The fiercest are foxes and wild cats, such the lynx, who prey on rabbits, mice, and other small animals. The wild boar is also ferocious,

Cork Oak

although it feeds only on vegetable matter.

The deciduous woodland's appearance changes with the seasons. In winter, tree branches are bare. In spring,

Temperate
Mediterranean
Boreal

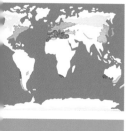

The temperate regions of the earth were once covered with trees, but most of the forests have been cleared to provide timber and to make way for farms, roads, and cities.

the leaves begin to bud as the temperature increases. The sun shines through the treetops, and flowers bloom on the forest floor. By summertime, the leaves are so broad that not enough sunlight penetrates for shrubs or flowers to grow under the canopy. The leaves of large trees—such as beech, oak, elm, chestnut, and ash—soak up the sun. The sunlight gives the trees energy, so that they can produce fruits and seeds. The leaves can make enough food to nourish the trees until spring. By autumn, the leaves are ready to drop. Before the leaves fall from the branches, they change from green to a magnificent array

Beech

branches do not break in heavy snow, because they bend easily and allow the snow to slip off.

DECIDUOUS TREES

Spring	Summer	Autumn	Winter

Great Fir

of reds and yellows. All year long, songbirds and small mammals find plenty of food and shelter among the trees.

In a coniferous, or boreal, forest, the trees grow tall and straight. Most conifers—such as pines, firs, and cedars—are conical in shape. Their evergreen leaves are like needles with a waxy coating, which prevents moisture loss and helps them to survive long periods of cold. Their

Almost one-third of the world's remaining forests are coniferous. Conifers are also grown in plantations to provide softwood for buildings, furniture, and paper.

LIFE IN THE TUNDRA

The tundra is a region of treeless plains in far northern North America, Europe, and Asia. For most of the year, the temperature stays below the freezing point. During the long, dark winter, icy winds blow and snow covers the ground. Summers are short and cool, but there is enough sunlight and heat for a carpet of low-growing plants to burst into flower and make their seeds.

The tundra plants are mostly grasses, mosses, lichens, and plants called sedges. They form small hills that hug the ground and can resist the wind. No trees grow because of the intensely cold winter winds and the permanently frozen soil, called permafrost, below the surface. The summer temperatures thaw only the top layer of soil, while the subsoil remains locked in ice. Because of the ice, the melted snow is unable to drain away, so the thawed summer soil is always wet. Hollows fill with water, which makes the landscape look like an immense meadow dotted with pools and streams. Caribou and reindeer leave their wintertime shelters in the coniferous forests. In herds many thousands strong, they return north to feast on the tundra's fresh green vegetation.

The main areas of tundra are around the Arctic Ocean, between the tree line and the region of perpetual ice around the pole. Tundra conditions also exist on high mountains.

PLANT LAYER

SOIL LAYER

PERMAFROST

Seasonal changes are spectacular on the tundra. The plants must complete an entire life cycle during a short growing season. Some grow, flower, and produce seeds within a month. Along with the herds that migrate, seabirds and waterfowl arrive to feed and nest among the new grass and flowers.

At the first sign of winter, the migrants head south. Only lemmings, arctic hares and foxes, and the sturdy musk oxen remain to live through the savage tundra winter. Many of these creatures are preyed upon by the polar bear, which comes south to hunt. When winter comes, the foxes and hares grow thick white coats, and the ptarmigans exchange their striped brown feathers for white ones. Their white winter coats camouflage them in the snow.

Because the tundra's climate is so forbidding and the land so unsuitable for

SUMMER

WINTER

Few animals can stay alive all year long in the tundra. The lemming survives in a labyrinth of tunnels under the snow, feeding on plant roots and shoots.

agriculture, it has been left largely unspoiled. Plans to mine the Arctic's rich deposits of oil, gas, iron ore, coal, and other minerals pose a threat, however. Already, a pipeline built to carry oil and gas scars the landscape. Because the vegetation recovers so slowly on the tundra, tracks made by vehicles forty years ago are still visible today.

MARSHES, SWAMPS, AND MANGROVES

Bog, marsh, swamp, and fen are some of the names given to wet, spongy land where the water level remains near or above the surface. Freshwater wetlands occur on the margins of lakes; in places where there is excess rainfall, melting snow, or flooding rivers; or where underground water reaches the surface. Saltwater wetlands, such as mangrove swamps, are found on coasts flooded by the sea.

Temperate wetlands are havens for water birds, particularly those that migrate. The white stork is one of the most spectacular migrants. After they spend the summer in the Low Countries of Belgium, the Netherlands, and Luxembourg, the storks fly south to warmer climates. They set off in autumn, and many pause to rest and feed in wetlands on the coasts of Spain and Portugal before they fly on to spend the winter in Africa.

Wetlands are found all over the world. Many of them are protected habitats, but others are in danger from developers who drain the land and build on it.

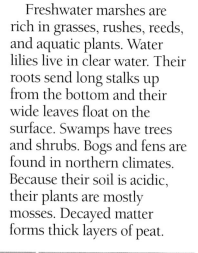

Freshwater marshes are rich in grasses, rushes, reeds, and aquatic plants. Water lilies live in clear water. Their roots send long stalks up from the bottom and their wide leaves float on the surface. Swamps have trees and shrubs. Bogs and fens are found in northern climates. Because their soil is acidic, their plants are mostly mosses. Decayed matter forms thick layers of peat.

Saltwater wetlands form in estuaries, where the tide rises high enough to flood the riverbanks. The river slows down as it meets the seawater. At high tide, the river overflows its banks. When the river overflows, it deposits mud and silt onto the mudflats by its banks. Carried by the wind, seeds of hardy *spartina* grass fall on the mud. When they germinate, their roots grow and form a network that spreads out and anchors the wet, shifting soil. As a result, *sea plantain* and other plants that are less tolerant of salt and of being submerged take up residence. Their roots bind the soil. Gradually, a community of plants is established that can cope with the general wetness and twice-daily floods of seawater.

Mangrove swamps are found on tropical coasts. Mangrove trees send down long, stilt like roots from their branches. The roots form a network that traps and binds mud and silt below the water and holds the branches and crown above it. The seeds often put out roots while the fruit is still on the tree. The seed root trails in the water, until the fruit falls in the water. Then, the root tip strikes mud and begins to grow a new tree. Mangrove swamps are home to many fish, birds, and the saltwater crocodile.

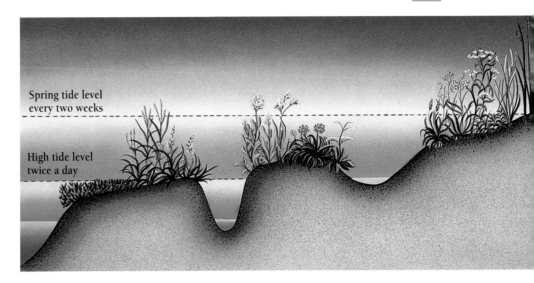

Spring tide level every two weeks

High tide level twice a day

Wetlands are a refuge for many animals, including the saltwater crocodile. Instead of being drained, many marshes are now being conserved.

CHANGING THE FACE OF THE LAND

There are few places left on earth that have not been changed by human beings. Landscapes that grew naturally over thousands of years are transformed in months or even weeks. In densely populated parts of the developed world, the natural vegetation has long since disappeared. It has been transformed into cities and farmland. Today, in many of the poorest parts of the world, this process is being repeated.

When the great tropical rain forest is cleared for cultivation, the land soon becomes infertile, and the soil is not suitable for growing crops or for pasture.

Huge tracts of tropical rain forest are felled every year for timber and to provide new farmland. People in these regions mistakenly believe that the forest soil is fertile, but in reality, the luxuriant growth of the forest results because the trees absorb nutrients before they can enrich the soil. When people grow crops on the cleared land, the soil is soon exhausted. Burning the forest down creates rough grazing land, but cattle quickly strip away the grass and shrubs that replace the trees. When new pasture is needed, the farmers move on to cut or burn down more trees. The cycle of rainforest destruction is repeated. The soil in the abandoned areas is left bare and unprotected. Heavy tropical rains form deep gullies and wash away the topsoil. In this way, tropical forest becomes wasteland.

Lightning causes some fires on the African savannas. Other fires are started deliberately by people, because they want to graze their animals there or to cultivate the land. Stripped of its natural vegetation, the land cannot support the wild animals. Because of the climate, crops do not thrive.

Goats strip the trees of their leaves, thereby killing them. When the rains come, they wash away the soil and turn the land into desert.

Precious forests are not only destroyed in these ways but are also killed by pollution. Power stations, factories, and cars pour out smoke that contains chemicals that turn into acid when dissolved in rain. This acid can be lethal for trees. The construction of taller

live in suburbs and shantytowns that grow in size and number. Towns and road systems in the developed world grow, too. People can travel for miles through the urban landscape and not see a patch of green.

All over the world, forests of buildings have replaced centuries-old forests of trees. People have transformed natural landscapes into artificial townscapes.

chimneys has allowed the winds to blow the smoke farther away, so that pollution from one country acidifies the rain that falls on forests in another.

During the twentieth century, a large number of people moved away from the land. In parts of the world where the soil is poor, farmers struggle to survive. Their children move to cities in search of work, where they

MAKING MOUNTAINS AND HABITATS

Use modeling clay to make a landscape. Shape the clay into three rectangles. Lay the rectangles on a board between two pieces of wood, then push the sides together. The layers of clay should fold upward to form mountains, in the same way that colossal pressures on layers of rock form real mountains.

Repeat the process with more clay, until you have a model landscape. You may have to work some of the clay into peaks and valleys with your fingers. If you want the mountains to look old and rounded, use sandpaper to imitate the action of the wind and rain. After you are finished, take your model outside or to a place that is waterproof. Use an spray bottle or hose to spray water over the mountains, so that it falls like rain.

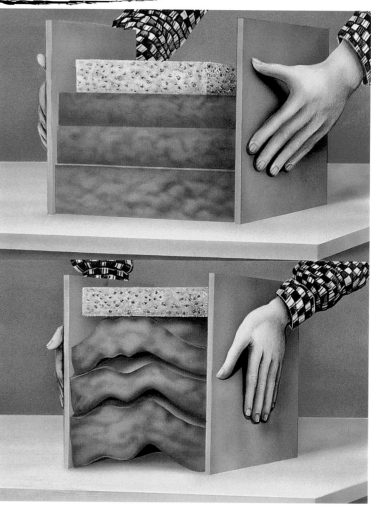

Watch the water as it runs down the mountainsides and collects in the valleys to form rivers. See how loose pieces of clay on the mountains are washed into the rivers and laid down on the flat land below. Once you are satisfied with the relief's appearance, let it dry. Use waterproof paints to paint blue rivers, green plains, and snowy white mountaintops on the model.

PLANT A MOUNTAIN

Make a second, larger model of a single mountain and the land around it. Then, paint the natural vegetation on it. Just as climate and vegetation change as you go from the equator to the poles, they also change as you go up a mountain. If the valleys and lowlands around your mountain are planted with crops, the lowest slopes of the mountain will have shrubs and deciduous trees on them, which will merge higher up the mountain into a band of coniferous trees. Then, at the tree line, the trees will stop and give way to alpine meadows, with plants that grow low to the ground like those of the tundra. Farther up the mountain, these plants will become scarcer, until, at last, the rocks are bare. Above the bare rocks, beyond the snow line, there is a region of perpetual ice and snow.

Snow and ice

Snow line

Bare rock

Alpine meadows

Deciduous trees

Farmland

CREATE A RAIN FOREST If you have a greenhouse, you can grow plants that are normally found only in a rain forest. For tropical orchids, you need to reproduce the hot, sticky climate. The best way to create a rainforest environment for orchids is to give them daily sunlight, provide a steady temperature above 73.4°F (23°C), and spray the leaves with water. Orchids can be expensive, so get advice from a good book or from an expert.

GLOSSARY

ADAPTATION Way in which animals and plants have evolved, both physically and in behavior, to survive in their environment.

ARMADILLO Small mammal that has bands of bony armor around its body.

ARROYO Dried-up riverbed that turns back into a river when it rains.

BISON Large wild ox, also called a buffalo in North America.

BLOCK MOUNTAIN Flat-topped mountain that has been forced up between parallel faults.

BOG Freshwater wetland with spongy, often peaty, ground.

BOREAL FOREST Coniferous forest.

CANOPY Dense leafy layer formed by the crowns (tops) of rainforest trees.

CONIFER Evergreen tree that bears cones and has needle-shaped leaves.

DECIDUOUS Describes any tree that sheds its leaves once a year.

DESERT Area with less than 9.75 inches (25 cm) of rain a year. Deserts can be hot or cold.

DORMANT Asleep or in a state of suspended animation.

DUNES Piles of sand created in deserts and on beaches by the wind.

EMERGENTS The tallest trees in a rain forest that reach above the canopy.

EPIPHYTE A plant that grows on another plant or surface but gets its nourishment from the atmosphere.

EQUATOR Imaginary line around the middle of the earth.

EQUATORIAL Region that lies close to the equator.

ERA Division of geological time. Eras are divided into periods.

EROSION Wearing down of the land.

ESTUARY Mouth of a river, where tidal salt water meets the river's freshwater.

FAULT Break in rocks, where one part has moved up, down, or sideways.

FEN Marshy land, often covered with water.

FLASH FLOOD Flood caused by sudden rain in an area too dry for the water to drain away slowly.

FOLD MOUNTAIN Mountain created by the collision of crustal plates.

FRESHWATER Water in lakes and rivers.

GEOLOGIST Scientist who studies rocks.

GLACIER River of ice formed by snow when it falls on mountains.

GRASSLAND Temperate region whose natural vegetation is grass.

GULLY Channel worn by running water.

HABITAT Place where certain animals and plants normally live.

HEMISPHERE Half of a sphere; used for the east–west and north–south halves of the earth.

HUMUS Rich part of the soil, formed from decayed living matter.

ICE AGE Any of several long periods during which the earth's climate was so cold that huge sheets of ice covered large areas of the northern and southern hemispheres.

LATITUDE North–south position of any point on earth, shown by lines on the map. Lines of longitude show the east–west position.

LAVA Magma that has been cast out by a volcano.

LIANA Any of several types of climbing plants that grow in the tropics.

LICHEN Plant that is a combination of a fungus and an alga and grows on rocks, trees, and other surfaces.

MANGROVE Tree found in swamps on tropical coasts.

MARSH Any area of wetland, such as a bog or fen.

MIGRATE To travel from one place to another, as wild deer, cattle, and many birds do every year in search of food.

MOUNTAIN Raised areas of land, generally 2,297 feet (700 m) or more above sea level. Lower uplands are called hills.

NUTRIENT Substance that provides nourishment for plants or animals.

OASIS Area of green in a desert where a spring or well gives a permanent water supply.

PAMPA Huge grassy plain in Argentina and other South American countries.

PEAT Decayed vegetable matter that builds up in wetlands. Over millions of years, it turns to coal.

PERIOD Part of an era in geological time.

PERMAFROST Ground that is always frozen.

PERMEABLE Able to allow water to pass through.

PLANTATION Land planted with a single crop, particularly trees.

PLATE One of eight large, and many small, pieces of the earth's crust.

POLE Point that marks the end (north or south) of the earth's axis, the imaginary line around which the planet spins.

PRAIRIE Grassy treeless plain of middle North America.

PREDOMINANT WIND Wind that blows most often from one direction.

PTARMIGAN A type of grouse that lives in the tundra. Its white feathers turn brown and red in summer.

RAIN FOREST Tropical forest made luxuriant by high temperatures and daily rainfall.

RELIEF Ups and downs of the land, shown on relief maps by contours, colors, or modeling.

RIFT VALLEY Deep valley caused when the land between two parallel faults sinks.

SALT WATER Water from the sea; water in lakes and rivers has no salt in it.

SAVANNA Tropical grassland with scattered trees, found between the rain forests and deserts in Africa, South America, Asia, and Australia.

SCRUB Land covered by stunted trees and shrubs.

SEDGE Grasslike plant with triangular stem that grows in marshes.

SNOW LINE Height above which there is permanent ice and snow on a mountain.

SOFTWOOD Timber from conifers; hardwood comes from deciduous trees and takes much longer to grow.

SPARTINA Kind of marsh grass that holds silt and builds up mud.

STEPPE Treeless grassy plain, particularly in Russia and Ukraine.

SWAMP Area of wet spongy land.

TEMPERATE Describes regions that are not too hot or too cold.

TREE LINE Height on the globe or on a mountain above which trees do not grow.

TROPICS Regions with warm or hot climates that lie north and south of the equator. These regions are bounded by two imaginary lines: the tropic of Cancer at 23 1/2° N and the tropic of Capricorn at 23 1/2° S.

TUNDRA Huge treeless plains in the Arctic and on the tip of South America. Tundra also occurs on mountains.

UNDERSTORY Trees, saplings, and shrubs that grow in a forest below the canopy.

VELD High grassy plains in southern Africa, with almost no trees.

WADI Desert riverbed that is dry most of the time.

WEATHERING Erosion by extremes of temperature and chemical action.

WETLANDS Areas of land that are almost submerged in water.

INDEX